Destination Detectives

Japan

North
America

Europe

Asia

Africa

JAPAN

South
America

Australasia

EXPRESS
EDITION

Jen Green

Raintree

Chicago, Illinois

Printed and bound in China
by South China Printing Company

10
10 9 8 7 6 5 4 3 2

Library of Congress Cataloging-in-Publication Data
Green, Jen.
  Japan / Jen Green.
    p. cm. -- (Destination detectives)
  Includes bibliographical references.
  ISBN 1-4109-2462-9 (lib. bdg.) –
  ISBN 1-4109-2469-6 (pbk.)
  ISBN 978-1-4109-2462-9 (lib. bdg.) –
  ISBN 978-1-4109-2469-8 (pbk.)
  1. Japan--Juvenile literature. I. Title. II. Series.
  DS806.G6 2006
  952--dc22
                              2005011558

This leveled text is a version of *Freestyle: Destination Detectives: Japan*

Acknowledgments
Alamy Images pp. 14–15 (A M Corporation), 16–17 (David Pearson), 39 (Hideo Kurihara); Corbis pp. 33 (B.S.P.I.), pp. 10–11, 11r (Bettmann), pp. 5t, 18–19 (Charles & Josette Lenars), 32 (David Samuel Robbins), pp. 21l , 41t (Free Agents Limited), pp. 5m, 26 (Kim Kyung-Hoon/Reuters), 30–31 (Kimimasa Mayama/Reuters), 34–35 (Michael Boys), 9 (Michael Maslan Historic Photographs), pp. 6, 14, 26–27, 36–37 (Michael S.Yamashita), 12–13 (Peter Guttman), pp. 13, 41b (Reuters), 28 (Richard T. Nowitz), 38 (Robert Essel NYC), 31t (Roger Ressmeyer), pp. 5b, 43b (Steve Kaufman), 8–9 (Werner Forman); Exile Images pp. 24–25 (J.Holmes); Getty Images p. 23 (Photodisc); Harcourt Education Ltd pp. 4r, 4l, 7, 17t, 20, 21r, 24t, 25t, 34, 36 (Debbie Rowe); JNTO pp. 18, 28–29, 42; Robert Harding Picture Library pp. 5 (Chris Rennie), 22 (P Koch); Travel-Ink p. 43t (Andy Lovell).

Cover photograph of colorful Japanese lanterns reproduced with permission of Corbis/ Michael S. Yamashita.

Illustrations by Kamae Design.

Every effort has been made to contact copyright holders of any material reproduced in this book. Any omissions will be rectified in subsequent printings if notice is given to the publishers.

The paper used to print this book comes from sustainable resources.

Disclaimer
All the Internet addresses (URLs) given in this book were valid at the time of going to press. However, due to the dynamic nature of the Internet, some addresses may have changed, or sites may have changed or ceased to exist since publication. While the author and publishers regret any inconvenience this may cause readers, no responsibility for any such changes can be accepted by either the author or the publishers.

Contents

Any words appearing in the text in bold, **like this,** are explained in the glossary. You can also look out for them in the Word Bank at the bottom of each page.

Where in the World?

You awake to find yourself snug on a mattress on the floor. You have never been in a room like this before. Straw mats cover the floor. There is very little furniture.

Out of the window, you see a small garden. It has a single tree and neatly raked gravel. Beyond the garden there is a park with cherry trees and a tall building. The building has a curved roof at each level. It is a **pagoda**.

Dangerous beauty

Beautiful Mount Fuji (pictured below) is Japan's most famous landmark. Fuji is also Japan's highest mountain. It is a volcano that has been quiet for 300 years.

Pagodas are towerlike temples. They have layers of graceful, curving roofs.

WORD BANK pagoda Japanese temple building

Welcome to Japan

What you thought was a wall turns out to be a screen. It slides back. Behind it stands a dark-haired girl of about your age. "*Yokoso* – welcome to Japan," she says. You are staying in a *minshuku*. This is a family home that takes paying guests. You are in the Japanese city of Kyoto.

Japanese homes are small and simply furnished. People sit on cushions around low tables.

Find out later...

...what **kabuki** is.

...how much an average **sumo** wrestler weighs.

...where these monkeys live.

5

An Island Nation

Japan at a glance

POPULATION:
127.4 million

AREA:
145,883 square miles (377,835 square kilometers)

CAPITAL:
Tokyo

OFFICIAL LANGUAGE:
Japanese.

Over breakfast the family you are staying with tells you about Japan. You look at a map together, and they show you some photos.

Four main islands

Japan is part of Asia. It lies in the northwest Pacific Ocean. Japan is made up of four main islands and many smaller ones. The main islands are Hokkaido, Honshu, Shikoku, and Kyushu.

Kyoto is on Honshu. Honshu is the largest Japanese island. It is often called the mainland.

Workers put together parts of a high-tech toilet. They work in one of Kyushu's modern factories.

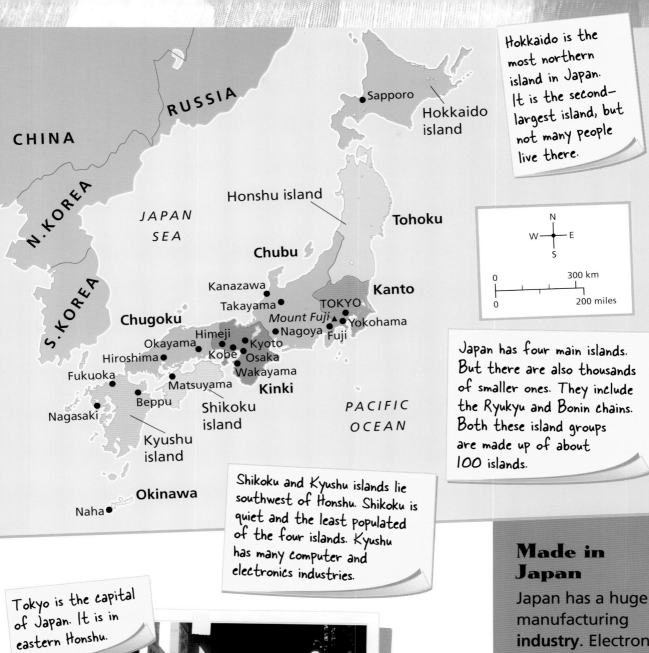

RUSSIA

CHINA

N. KOREA

S. KOREA

JAPAN SEA

Sapporo

Hokkaido island

Tohoku

Honshu island

Chubu

Kanto

Kanazawa

Takayama

TOKYO

Yokohama

Chugoku

Himeji

Mount Fuji

Nagoya

Fuji

Okayama

Kyoto

Hiroshima

Kobe

Osaka

Fukuoka

Wakayama

Matsuyama

Kinki

Beppu

Shikoku island

PACIFIC OCEAN

Nagasaki

Kyushu island

Okinawa

Naha

Hokkaido is the most northern island in Japan. It is the second-largest island, but not many people live there.

N
W E
S

0   300 km

0   200 miles

Japan has four main islands. But there are also thousands of smaller ones. They include the Ryukyu and Bonin chains. Both these island groups are made up of about 100 islands.

Shikoku and Kyushu islands lie southwest of Honshu. Shikoku is quiet and the least populated of the four islands. Kyushu has many computer and electronics industries.

Tokyo is the capital of Japan. It is in eastern Honshu.

Made in Japan

Japan has a huge manufacturing **industry**. Electronic goods are manufactured, or made, in Japan. They are sold all around the world. Japanese cars and motorcycles are also very popular in many countries.

History

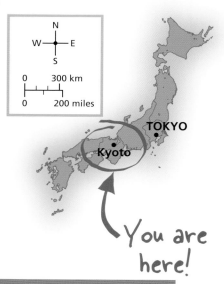

You are here!

Kyoto is an ancient city full of amazing buildings. After breakfast you look through a tourist brochure. It gives you a short guide to Japan's history.

Emperors and shoguns

Japan's first emperor united the country 1,600 years ago. This happened in about C.E. 400. **Shoguns** ruled Japan from the 1190s until the 1860s. They ruled for more than 670 years. Shoguns were powerful military leaders. During this period, the emperors had no real power.

Kyoto

In C.E. 794 an emperor named Kammu founded the city of Kyoto. Kyoto was Japan's capital for over 1,000 years. In the 1860s Tokyo became the new capital.

Nijo Castle is one of Kyoto's most beautiful buildings. It was built in 1603 by a famous shogun named Tokugawa Ieyasu.

➤

WORD BANK shogun Japanese military leader. Shoguns ruled Japan for more than 670 years.

Isolation

For the last 200 years of their rule, the shoguns stopped all contact between Japan and the rest of the world. They thought this would prevent other countries from invading. Japan was totally cut off from the rest of the world.

Samurai warriors

Shoguns and other powerful landowners kept armies of warriors called **samurai**. The samurai lived according to strict rules. Honor was very important to them. A samurai would prefer to kill himself than **surrender** in battle.

This picture of samurai warriors was taken in the 1890s. They are carrying long swords and wearing thick armor.

surrender give yourself up to the enemy

End of isolation

In 1853 the United States sent a fleet of warships to Japan. This led Japan to renew contact with other countries.

Change quickly followed. Powerful Japanese landowners defeated the **shogun**. They then made the sixteen-year-old Emperor Meiji the new ruler. Japan began to modernize. It had to catch up with Europe and the United States.

In about 1900 Japan began building an **empire**. It took over other lands in Asia.

► This old picture shows the U.S. Navy arriving in Japan in 1853.

WORD BANK   empire group of countries controlled by one country

Recent years

World War II began in Europe in 1939. In 1941 Japanese bombers attacked the U.S. Navy at Pearl Harbor. Pearl Harbor is in Hawaii. Japan had entered the war.

In 1945 the United States dropped **atomic bombs** on two Japanese cities. They were Hiroshima and Nagasaki. The atomic bomb was a weapon of mass destruction. Many people were hurt or killed. Japan **surrendered**.

At the end of World War II, the country lay in ruins. But it quickly recovered. In just twenty years, Japan became a top industrial nation.

Kamikaze pilots

During World War II, Japanese **kamikaze** pilots flew planes into U.S. ships. These pilots knew they would die in these attacks. The planes were often packed with explosives. A total of 34 ships were sunk by kamikaze attacks.

◄ The USS *Bunker Hill* was badly damaged during World War II. It was hit by a kamikaze bomb on June 21, 1945.

atomic bomb extremely destructive bomb (powered by the release of nuclear energy)

Climate and Geography

From Kyoto you take the cable car up to nearby Mount Hiei. The view from the top is fantastic. You talk to the other people there about Japan.

The land

Japan is a long, slim country. It stretches about 1,500 miles (2,500 kilometers) from north to south. You are never far from the sea. Most of inland Japan is mountainous. Towns, factories, and farms are on the flat areas or **plains**. They are around the coasts.

> ➤
> Cable cars
> transport people
> up into the
> mountains of
> Honshu.

WORD BANK   erupt to release lava and ash

Volcanoes and earthquakes

The Japanese are used to volcanoes and earthquakes. Japan has over 60 active volcanoes. They sometimes **erupt** clouds of ash and red-hot **lava**. Small earthquakes often occur, but people hardly notice them. Major earthquakes cause huge destruction.

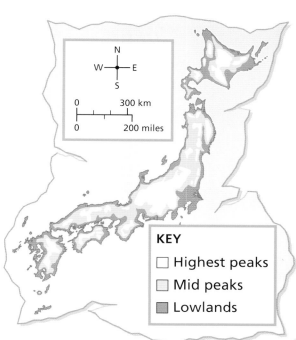

N
W — E
S

0   300 km

0   200 miles

KEY

☐ Highest peaks

☐ Mid peaks

▨ Lowlands

Deadly earthquakes

Japan's worst earthquake disaster was the Great Kanto Earthquake of 1923. Over 100,000 people died. In 1995 a major earthquake rocked the city of Kobe in southwest Honshu. It killed more than 6,300 people.

Crushed cars are pulled from under a collapsed highway. The collapse happened during the Kobe earthquake of 1995.

lava hot, liquid rock that comes out of a volcano

Climate

It is springtime. The days here are mild and sunny. But have you got the right clothes for visiting the rest of Japan?

Different parts of the country have different weather. Hokkaido is in the far north. It has long, snowy winters and short, cool summers. Central Japan has warm summers and cool winters. The weather in the far south is much hotter.

Early spring is *hanami* season. This is when people celebrate the blossoming of the cherry trees. Families and friends go for picnics under the fruit trees.

WORD BANK   typhoon tropical spinning storm that brings high winds and torrential rain

Changing seasons

Japan's seasons fall at about the same time as seasons in the United States and Europe. The sunny weather in early spring is followed by a rainy season. Fall sometimes brings hurricanes called **typhoons** (see panel on right).

Winds called **monsoons** sometimes blow across Japan. In summer the monsoons bring rain to southern and central areas. In winter they bring rain and snow to the north and west.

Typhoons

Tropical storms called **typhoons** (hurricanes) strike Japan between July and November. These huge, spinning storms begin out in the Pacific Ocean. They then sweep inland. Tyhoons bring winds of over 124 miles (200 kilometers) per hour. Heavy rains flatten crops and cause floods.

Okinawa is an island in the Ryukyu chain of southern Japan. It never gets cold enough for frosts here.

monsoon wind that brings heavy rainfall to southern Asia

Food and Culture

After your trip up Mount Hiei, you're really hungry. The restaurant you go to is very busy. Japanese people often entertain their guests by eating out instead of cooking at home.

The three Os

Eating out in Japan, you're sure to meet the three Os. *Oshibori* are small, damp cloths to wipe your hands and face. *O-hashi* are chopsticks. These are used instead of knives and forks. At the end of the meal, you'll be served a refreshing green tea called *o-cha*.

Rice with everything

Rice is the most important food in Japan. It is eaten at most meals. The Japanese also eat a lot of fish. In dishes such as sashimi, fish is eaten raw. But this has to be high-quality fresh fish.

► These men are slurping noodles (*soba*), in a Tokyo noodle bar.

16

In the past the Japanese ate very little meat or dairy products. Now they eat more of these foods. This is because the Japanese diet is becoming more like European or U.S. diets.

Slurping noodles

Noodles served in a hot soup make a filling meal. Table manners are very important in Japan. But it is OK to make loud slurping sounds when you eat noodles.

➤ Sushi is a popular type of food in Japan. It is cakes of rice topped with raw or cooked fish, vegetables, or seaweed.

Gift ideas

Traditional arts and crafts in Japan make great gifts. They include:

- *Daruma* dolls: **papier-mâché** statues. They are thought to bring good luck.
- *Netsuke*: carved toggles. These buttonlike fasteners were traditionally made of ivory.
- Lacquerware: bowls and boxes painted with tree sap. This hardens to a glossy sheen.

Out and about

The next day you set off early to explore the city of Kyoto. You want to find out what Japanese cities have to offer.

First, you have breakfast at a coffee shop. You decide on a traditional breakfast. This is boiled rice, dried fish, seaweed, soybean soup, and pickles. When you've finished, you go off in search of souvenirs in Gion. Gion is Kyoto's main shopping district.

A traditional Japanese lacquerware bowl.
▼

WORD BANK papier-mâché material made from strips of paper mixed with paste. It is molded into shape when wet and hardens as it dries.

High drama

How do the Japanese enjoy themselves in the city? Many visit a *pachinko* (pinball) parlor. Others might go to a **kabuki** play.

Kabuki is a traditional form of Japanese theater. It is a mix of **opera,** dance, and music. All the performers are men. People get very involved in the action. They cheer the heroes and boo the villains.

Two actors perform a *kabuki* play. These plays are about passion, jealousy, and revenge.

opera drama that is set to music. Performers sing their words instead of speaking them.

Shinto shrines

The entrance to a Shinto shrine is marked by a special gateway. This gateway is called a *torii*. Visitors **purify** themselves by rinsing their mouths and hands with water.

Religion

You pay a visit to Kyoto's beautiful Kinkakuji temple. Another visitor there talks to you about Japanese beliefs and festivals.

Shinto is Japan's oldest religion. People believe that gods called *kami* live in rivers, lakes, mountains, and other natural places.

Buddhism is another ancient religion. It came to Japan about 1,500 years ago. Buddhism teaches that true happiness is found through wisdom and understanding. Most Japanese people follow both Shinto and Buddhism.

Festivals

There are festivals every month of the year in Japan. Children's Day is on May 5. This is when children fly kites in the shape of carp fish. Girls' Day falls on March 3. On this day, girls dress their favorite dolls in little silk **kimonos** (see page 21).

This is a *torii* entrance to a Shinto shrine.

WORD BANK   purify cleanse or make something clean

Kimonos

Kimonos (see picture below) are silk robes tied at the waist with a sash. Few people now wear kimonos every day. But men and women wear them for special occasions.

This is Kyoto's Kinkakuji, or Temple of the Golden Pavilion. It was built by a **shogun** in the 1300s. It is covered with a thin layer of gold leaf.

torii wooden gateway that marks the entrance to a Shinto shrine

Everyday Life

Team spirit

Team spirit is very important to Japanese companies. Everyone eats together in the same cafeteria and wears the same uniform.

During your stay at the *minshuku*, you notice that the father always works late. The family tells you that many Japanese people work long hours. They often work six days a week and take just one or two weeks' vacation each year.

A job for life?

In the past, Japanese workers expected to work for the same company until they **retired**. But this is changing. Now people change jobs more often.

Factory workers stretch and exercise together before starting work in the morning.

▶

WORD BANK   retire to stop working, usually because of age

The working day

Loyalty and politeness are very important in Japanese companies. The day begins with workers bowing to one another. People also bow to show thanks or to say they are sorry. The workers do exercises together and sing the company song. Then everyone settles down to work.

After work

After a long day at the office, Japanese workers often spend the evening together. They may visit an *izakaya*. An *izakaya* is a cross between a restaurant and a bar. They may go to a bar for a **karaoke** evening. Here, people can sing along to recorded music.

This woman is performing in a karaoke club in Tokyo.

karaoke form of entertainment, involving singing to recorded music

School days

The family you're staying with has two children of school age. They always seem to be doing homework. You ask them about school in Japan.

Japanese children have to go to school between the ages of six and fifteen. About 90 percent of them will continue their studies at a senior high school. One out of three will go on to college or university after that.

These *Kanji* characters make the words "autumn star."

Japanese writing

Japanese children have to learn four writing systems. *Kanji* is the main script. It has thousands of symbols for making words.

These Japanese schoolgirls are studying English.

martial art ancient form of self-defense

Working hard

Children go to school from Monday through Friday. Their day begins at 8:30 A.M. and finishes at 4:30 P.M.

After school, pupils spend one or two hours doing homework. They also have exams about six times a year. Before exams many pupils take extra lessons at private schools called *juku*. No wonder the time before exams is stressful!

Playing hard

Children practice sports as part of their school education. Most children also learn one form of **martial art** at school. Martial arts are ancient forms of self-defense. Judo (see picture above), karate, or **kendo** (fencing) are all martial arts.

Sumo wrestling

Sumo is an ancient Japanese sport. Each *rikishi* (wrestler) tries to force his opponent out of the ring. Or, he tries to make his opponent touch the ground with any part of his body other than his feet.

Time off

What do Japanese people do after working hard all day? You ask your host family about sports and leisure in Japan.

Lots of Japanese watch and play sports. The national sports are **sumo** wrestling (see panel on the left) and baseball. Soccer became very popular in the 1990s. Many Japanese also enjoy golfing. Martial arts such as karate, judo, and **kendo** were invented in Japan.

The average *rikishi* weighs over 326 pounds (150 kilograms). Wrestlers eat a special diet to put on weight.

WORD BANK   sumo form of traditional wrestling in Japan

Leisure and hobbies

Many Japanese people like gardening. In crowded cities, people take great care of their small yard or window box. **Bonsai** are miniature trees. These can be grown indoors.

Purikura (print club) machines are very popular with children. These machines take photos of children and their friends in fun poses. The photos are made into tiny stickers that people put everywhere!

Bonsai trees grow less than 3 feet (1 meter) tall. The tiny branches are carefully trimmed and wired to make a beautiful shape.

bonsai art of growing miniature trees, a traditional pastime in Japan

Travel and Cities

Speeding bullets

Japan's "bullet trains," or *shinkansen*, race at 170 miles (275 kilometers) per hour between cities. The Kyoto to Tokyo line stretches between Kyushu in the south to northern Honshu.

You've had a few days in Kyoto. Now you want to see more of Japan. You go to the tourist office to ask about the best way to travel.

Air travel

Japan has over 170 airports. There is very little flat land in Japan. Because of this, some airports are built on artificial islands in the sea. Osaka airport is one of them.

Some bullet trains have two decks. Seats on the top deck are more expensive. They even have their own televisions.

WORD BANK   *shinkansen* Japan's high-speed trains, also called "bullet trains"

Road and rail

Japan has a modern road network. Most roads run around the coast. Some roads go through tunnels under the mountains.

There are different types of trains in Japan. You pay more to ride the faster trains. The Maglev is the newest. It has no wheels. Instead, powerful magnets allow the Maglev train to float above the rail.

The Akashi Kaikyo Bridge links Honshu and Shikoku Islands. It is the world's longest suspension bridge. A suspension bridge has a roadway that hangs from cables.

You are here!

Tokyo – Japan's capital

The bullet train brings you smoothly into Tokyo Station. You are now in Japan's capital. Ten percent of Japan's population lives here.

Eastern capital

Tokyo was the home of the **shoguns** that ruled Japan for centuries. Today Tokyo's architecture is mainly modern. Most old buildings have been destroyed. They were destroyed by an earthquake or by bombs during World War II.

Tokyo fact file

POPULATION:
12.06 million (in 2000)

AREA:
844 square miles (2,187 square kilometers)

DATE FOUNDED:
1457, when it was named Edo.

➤ Ginza is Tokyo's most famous shopping district. It is also an entertainment area with many restaurants, cafés, and clubs.

shogun Japanese military leader. Shoguns ruled Japan for more than 670 years.

Sightseeing in Tokyo

Many of Tokyo's top sights are just a short way from the station. The Imperial Palace is the emperor's home. Its grounds hold the National Museum of Modern Art and the Science Museum.

To the north you will find Ueno Park. This large park has a zoo and a boating lake. It also has some of Tokyo's top museums.

"Rooms" in a capsule hotel are very cozy! There's just space for a bed and a television screen.

Capsule hotels

Space is very cramped in the center of Tokyo. Some hotels have rooms the size of big lockers. These are called "capsule hotels." The rooms measure just 6 feet (2 meters) long, 3 feet (1 meter) wide, and 3 feet (1 meter) tall.

Island shrine

The island shrine of Miyajima lies in the bay at Hiroshima. The island is a **holy** site. The curving gateway, or *torii*, is one of Japan's most famous sights.

Japan's cities

You've visited Tokyo, but Japan has many other great cities. There's Sapporo on the island of Hokkaido. It is a great place for skiing. Nara is an ancient city in central Honshu. It has hundreds of temples.

Some tourists visit Hiroshima in western Honshu. The city was destroyed by an **atomic bomb** in 1945 (see page 11). A flame burns in Hiroshima's Peace Park. It will only be put out when all nuclear weapons have been destroyed.

Miyajima's famous "floating gateway" stands in the bay at Hiroshima.

WORD BANK   atomic bomb extremely destructive bomb (powered by the release of nuclear energy)

Old and new in Osaka

You decide to visit Osaka in southern Honshu. This is Japan's third-largest city. It has a beautiful castle from the 1500s. Nearby, Panasonic Square attracts lots of young people. The latest computer games are on display there. You try one of the games. Then you take a boat trip along the city's waterways.

You are here!

TOKYO

Osaka

N
W — E
S

0   300 km

0   200 miles

Puppet theater

Osaka is home to the National Bunraku Theater. *Bunraku* is a form of puppet theater. The puppeteers are very skillful. They make the puppets move in a very realistic and graceful way.

Like many Japanese cities, Osaka is a mixture of the old and new. Gleaming skyscrapers tower over the old castle.

torii wooden gateway that marks the entrance to a Shinto shrine

Urban life

In Osaka you decide to stay in another *minshuku*. Staying with a family seems a good way to get to know a city.

Crowded centers

More than three-quarters of Japan's population live in towns or cities. Like Tokyo, Osaka's streets can get very crowded and jammed with traffic. The best way to get to work is to walk or cycle to the nearest train station. Then you take a train.

City homes

Homes in city centers are often small. A family with two children usually lives in an apartment with just four rooms.

No one wears shoes indoors. Outdoor shoes are always left in the hallway. People wear slippers or socks in the house. There are special slippers for wearing in the bathroom.

Bath time

Bath time in Japan is a soak in a bathtub full of piping-hot water. But you soap yourself down or shower before getting into the tub. This is because the whole family takes turns using the tub.

This is a traditional Japanese bedroom. People usually sleep on **futons**. These are mattresses that can be rolled up when not in use.

Rural Life

Family sizes

Japanese families used to be much larger than they are now. Parents, children, and grandparents lived together. The grandparents looked after the children while the parents worked. This still happens in the countryside. But it rarely happens in cities.

You are here!

It's time for a change from city life. You decide to spend a few days in the country. You head for the village of Ogimachi in the Japan Alps. You decide to stay in a traditional inn called a *ryokan*.

This large family lives together in rural Japan.

A mountain village

In the village of Ogimachi the houses are tall. The roofs are made of dry straw or reeds. These roofs are steep so snow can slide off them. The air here is clear and cold.

Plans for the future

You hire a bicycle to explore the countryside. You meet a group of schoolchildren. You chat with them about what they plan to do when they finish school. Some want to escape to a big city. Others want to stay in the country. Many people today can work at home wherever they live. This is because of the Internet and other new technology.

Keeping warm

The climate in the mountains is colder than in the lowlands. In winter people sit around a low table with a heater underneath. They warm their legs under a quilt that covers the table.

People live on the first floor of these tall village houses. The top floor is usually used for storage and craftwork.

Silk farming

In central Honshu people raise silkworms in mulberry orchards. The silkworms spin silken cocoons. They do this just before they change from caterpillars to moths. These threads are then gathered and woven to make silk.

Farming and fishing

Ogimachi sits in a narrow **valley**. The bottom of the valley is filled with gardens, rice fields, and flower plots.

Most fields in Japan are small. A lot of the farming is done on weekends. Farmers often work in offices and factories during the week. Rice is the main crop. It is grown in special **paddy fields.** These are fields that are kept flooded with water. Farmers also grow wheat, barley, tobacco, vegetables, tea, and fruits.

The land on this hillside has been stepped or terraced. This creates lots of small, flat fields. These are used for growing rice.

valley low land between hills or mountains

Fishing industry

Fish, shellfish, and seaweed make up a major part of the Japanese diet. Because of this, fishing is very important. Japan has one of the largest fishing fleets in the world.

Japanese fishing boats search local waters and the world's oceans for fish and shellfish. Japanese farmers breed carp and trout in tanks. Breeding fish means that the farmers raise fish for food. Also, fish farms around the coasts breed bream and tuna.

These Japanese fishing boats are in a harbor in Kyushu.

paddy field field used to grow rice, which can be flooded at certain times of the year

Tourism and Travel

In Ogimachi you chat with the other guests in the inn. They tell you about places to visit in Japan.

Island attractions

So far, you've only seen parts of mainland Honshu. But each island has its own attractions. Hokkaido in the north has large wilderness areas. In the south, Shikoku is famous for its temples. Kyushu has active volcanoes and hot springs.

National parks – some attractions

- Daisetsuzan, Hokkaido: great hiking country
- Fuji-Hakone-Izu, Honshu: lakes, beaches, and volcanoes, including Mount Fuji
- Inland Sea between Honshu and Shikoku: rugged coastline, pine-covered islands.

The Japan Alps in Hokkaido are popular with hikers, climbers, and skiers.

Kanazawa on the Sea of Japan is an artists' community.

Okinawa in the Ryukyu chain of islands is great for snorkeling. It is also the home of karate. You can have a training session or watch a display of this **martial art**.

Nagasaki on Kyushu is a historic seaport.

Beppu on Kyushu and Matsuyama on Shikoku are **spa** resorts. There are natural hot springs.

Hokkaido

Sapporo

SEA OF JAPAN

Honshu

Kanazawa

Himeji

Matsuyama

Kyushu

Nagasaki   Beppu   **Shikoku**

Aso-Kujuu

INLAND SEA

Fuji-Hakone-Izu

Okinawa

N
W · E
S

0   300 km
0   200 miles

spa   resort where there are mineral springs or baths

Natural wonders

Japan's national parks protect areas of natural beauty. These include volcanoes, hot springs, crater lakes, wetlands, coastlines, and remote islands.

The Ryukyu and Bonin island chains are in the far south. They have warm and wet weather. There are sandy beaches and clear blue waters. Many people go there for snorkeling.

The Castle of the White Crane at Himeji, in western Honshu, is one of Japan's most beautiful castles.

Sapporo, Hokkaido, is a winter sports center. In February, the Snow Festival here features amazing ice and snow sculptures.

Stay or Go Home?

Hot springs

Take a dip in one of Japan's famous *onsen* (hot springs). These are usually found close to volcanoes. The warm, bubbling waters are good for aches and pains.

You have visited Kyoto, Tokyo, and Osaka. You've seen the countryside around Ogimachi. But there is still lots more to do. Do you stay or do you head for home?

Snow sports

Your friends at the inn make a list of things you should do. At the top of the list is snowboarding or skiing. You can do this in the Japan Alps in central Honshu or on Hokkaido.

▶ Snowboarding in Hokkaido is becoming a very popular pastime.

Wildlife and hiking

The island of Shodo-shima is in the Inland Sea. You should go there to see the wild macaques, or snow monkeys, showing off. Special wildlife parks have been set up around Japan to protect the snow monkeys.

Many Japanese aim to climb Mount Fuji once in their lifetimes. The climbing season is July and August. You can hike all the way up. Or you can cheat by taking the bus halfway.

These macaques are bathing in a hot spring. They have learned that this is a good way to warm up in freezing-cold weather.

The tea ceremony

Going to a tea ceremony (see picture above) can be a calming experience. The ceremony takes place in a tea pavilion that overlooks a beautiful garden. Guests chat while the hostess prepares special green tea.

Find Out More

World Wide Web

If you want to find out more about Japan, you can search the Internet. Try using keywords such as these:

- Japan
- Shinano River
- Tokyo

You can also find your own keywords by using words from this book. Try using a search directory such as: **yahooligans.com**.

Are there ways for a Destination Detective to find out more about Japan? Yes! Check out the books and movies listed below:

Further reading

Dean, Arlan. *Samurai: Warlords of Japan.* Danbury, Conn.: Children's Press, 2005.

Green, Jen. *Nations of the World: Japan.* Chicago: Raintree, 2001.

Haslam, Andrew. *Make It Work: Japan.* Minnetonka, Minn.: Two-Can Publishing, 2000.

Kalman, Bobbie. *Japan: The People.* New York: Crabtree Publishing, 2002.

Richardson, Hazel. *Life in Ancient Japan.* New York: Crabtree Publishing, 2005.

Movies

Spirited Away (2001) This animated film is about a miserable ten-year-old girl who is moving to a new house. She stumbles into the mysterious world of the Japanese gods.

The Seven Samurai (1953) This classic action film tells a story about Japanese warriors in the 1500s.

Time Line

around C.E. 400
The powerful Yamoto family unite Japan. They become Japan's emperors.

552
Buddhism reaches Japan.

794
Kyoto becomes the capital of Japan.

1192
Yoritomo becomes the first **shogun**. He is head of the Minamoto clan.

1543
Portuguese sailors are the first Europeans to visit Japan.

1603
Tokugawa Ieyasu becomes shogun. The Tokugawa clan remains in power for the next 264 years. They rule Japan from Edo (now Tokyo).

1630s
Japan cuts off all contact with the outside world.

1853–1854
Commodore Matthew Perry of the United States persuades Japan to renew contact with the outside world.

1868
The rule of the shoguns is overthrown. The power of Japan's emperors is restored. Emperor Meiji begins his rule. Tokyo becomes the capital of Japan.

1894–1895
Japan wins a war against China over Korea.

1905
Japan wins a war against Russia.

1923
The Great Kanto Earthquake devastates Tokyo, Yokohama, and other cities on the Kanto Plain.

1937
Japan invades China.

1941
Japan bombs U.S. ships at Pearl Harbor in Hawaii. By doing this, Japan enters World War II on the side of Germany. The United States enters the war on the opposite side.

1945
Japan **surrenders** after U.S. aircraft drop **atomic bombs** on the cities of Hiroshima and Nagasaki. U.S. and other Allied forces take over Japan.

1952
US and Allied forces withdraw from Japan.

1960s
Japan's economy booms.

1995
The Kobe earthquake kills over 6,300 people.

1998
The Winter Olympics are held in Nagano.

2002
The World Cup finals are co-hosted by Japan and Korea.

Japan – Facts and Figures

The Japanese flag has a white background with a red circle in the center. The white represents honesty and purity. The red disc is a sun symbol meaning brightness, honesty, and warmth.

People and places

- Population: 127.4 million.
- Mount Aso National Park on the small island of Jumamoto is one of the world's largest areas of volcanic activity.

What's in a name?

- Japan's official name is *Nippon*, or *Nihon*. This means "Source of the Sun."
- The national flag of Japan is known as the *Nisshohki* or *Hinomaru*. This means "sun disc."

Money matters

- Japan's economic output is huge, second only to the United States.
- The Japanese currency is the yen.

Food facts

- The average Japanese person eats more than 154 pounds (69 kilograms) of fish per year. This is almost half a pound (227 grams) per day!
- Never stick chopsticks upright into your bowl of rice. This is how food is offered to the dead.

Glossary

atomic bomb extremely destructive bomb (powered by the release of nuclear energy)

bonsai art of growing miniature trees, a traditional pastime in Japan

Buddhism religion founded in India by Siddhartha Gautama in 525 B.C.E. Buddhism later spread to many parts of Asia.

empire group of countries controlled by one country

erupt to release lava and ash

futon mattress that can be rolled up when not in use

holy associated with a divine power

industry businesses that provide a particular service

kabuki lively form of drama using music, song, and dance. *Kabuki* dates back to the 1600s.

kamikaze type of Japanese pilot in World War II. They used their airplanes as bombs to attack enemies.

karaoke form of entertainment, involving singing to recorded music

kendo martial art of fencing, using bamboo swords

kimono robe with wide sleeves, which is the traditional dress of Japanese men and women

lava hot, liquid rock that comes out of a volcano

martial art ancient form of self-defense

minshuku Japanese home that takes paying guests

monsoon wind that brings heavy rainfall to southern Asia

opera drama that is set to music. Performers sing their words instead of speaking them.

paddy field field used to grow rice, which can be flooded at certain times of the year

pagoda Japanese temple building

papier-mâché material made from strips of paper mixed with paste. It is molded into shape when wet and hardens as it dries.

plain flat area, sometimes near the coast

purify cleanse or make something clean

retire to stop working, usually because of age

samurai Japanese warrior in the time of the shoguns

shinkansen Japan's high-speed trains, also called "bullet trains"

Shinto ancient Japanese religion, meaning "way of the gods"

shogun Japanese military leader. Shoguns ruled Japan for more than 670 years.

spa resort where there are mineral springs or baths

sumo form of traditional wrestling in Japan

surrender give yourself up to the enemy

torii wooden gateway that marks the entrance to a Shinto shrine

typhoon tropical spinning storm that brings high winds and torrential rain

valley low land between hills or mountains

Index